SA

tiersen

Published by

Chester Music
part of The Music Sales Group
14-15 Berners Street, London W1T 3LJ, UK.

All music by Yann Tiersen.
© Copyright 2015 Everything's Calm Music under
exclusive licence to Chester Music Limited.
All Rights Reserved. International Copyright Secured.

Exclusive Distributors:
Music Sales Limited
Distribution Centre, Newmarket Road,
Bury St Edmunds, Suffolk IP33 3YB, UK.

Music Sales Corporation
180 Madison Avenue, 24th Floor,
New York, NY 10016, USA.

Music Sales Pty Limited
Level 4, Lisgar House,
30-32 Carrington Street,
Sydney, NSW 2000 Australia.

Order No. CH84227
ISBN 978-1-78558-131-1
This book © Copyright 2015 Chester Music Limited.
All Rights Reserved.

Photographs by Emilie Quinquis.
Music engraved and processed by Paul Ewers Music Design.
Cover design by Vitamin P.

Printed in the EU.

INTRODUCTION

Two years ago I was travelling through California by bicycle
with my fiancée. One day we were cycling along a remote track
of the Lost Coast in the middle of the Sinkyone Wilderness
State Park. It wasn't an easy trip — we were alone, with
no humans nearby and no noise around. After five hours of
cycling we heard a sound to our left; something was moving
in the undergrowth beside the path. The noises continued as
we cycled on until, after half an hour, we saw a mountain
lion cross the path ahead of us. This big and beautiful
cat was obviously looking for lunch and had been circling
us all afternoon. We cycled for hours until we eventually
reached safety.

Our lives changed completely after this event. On this
special day on the Californian Lost Coast I was nothing more
than food for a wild animal. It made me realise that where
we are at any given place is integral to who we are. Our
place in the world is what defines us more than anything.
And it made me feel that I needed to know more deeply my
own place, my own home, to discover who I am.

And my home is the island of Ushant, West Brittany, in the
middle of the Celtic Sea. To understand it and to discover
myself I decided to draw a musical map of the island. Here
is Volume One: ten piano works about ten places on Ushant
with ten pictures by my fiancée, and a link to ten field
recordings from those places.

Listen to the field recordings at **www.eusasound.bzh**

DIGORADUR

Daou vloaz zo e oan o foetañ bro e Kalifornia war varc'h-houarn gant va danvez-pried. An deiz-se e oamp o veajiñ war un hent distro e-kreiz Sinkyone Wilderness State Park, an "aod kollet", e kornôg Kalifornia. Ne oa ket ur valeadenn aes. Hon-unan edomp, ne oa na den na trouz. Goude pemp eurvezh war varc'h-houarn hor boa klevet trouzioù treid a-gleizdeomp hag aet e oamp gant an trouzioù-se e-pad un hantereurvezh. A-benn ar fin hor boa gwelet ur puma, bras ha brav. O klask boued e verenn edo. Boued puma e oamp bet ar wech-se war "aod kollet" Kalifornia!

Hor buhez zo cheñchet goude-se.

Ma c'hellan bezañ boued ahont eo ret din anaout va bro evit dizoleiñ piv on amañ, ha "piv on amañ" eo "piv on", rak amañ emaon atav.

War Enez Eusa emaon o chom ha graet em eus va soñj da gregiñ gant ur gartenn-sonerezh eus an enez.

Setu al levrenn gentañ, enni dek pezh piano diwar dek lec'h, luc'hskeudennoù gant Emilie Kinkiz, hag ul liamm evit selaou dek enrolladenn eus al lec'hioù-se.

Setu al liamm evit selaou an enroladennoù: www.eusasound.bzh

PERN

48° 26' 51"N 5° 8' 27"W

PERN

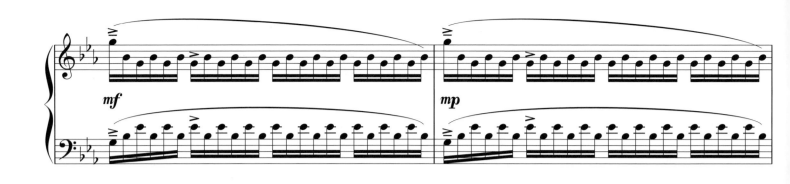

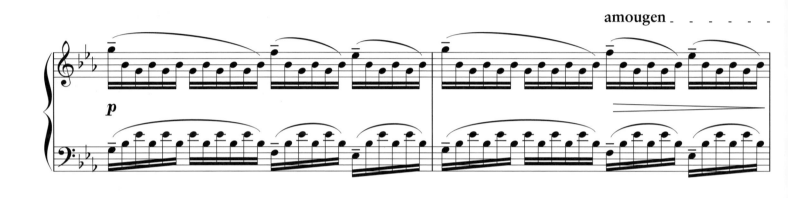

amougen _ . . . . . .

Reollusk

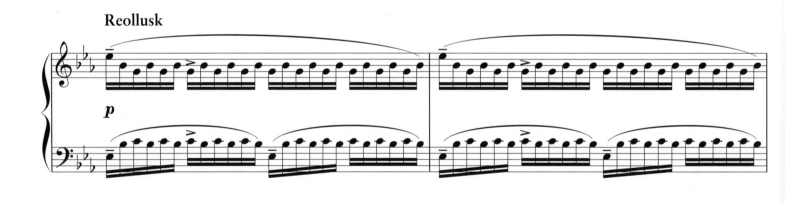

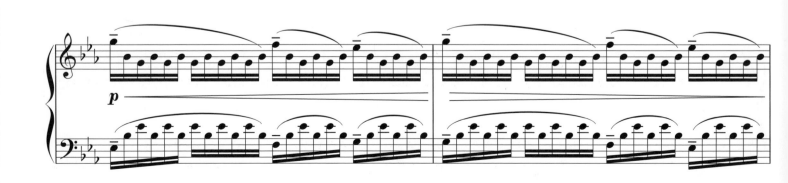

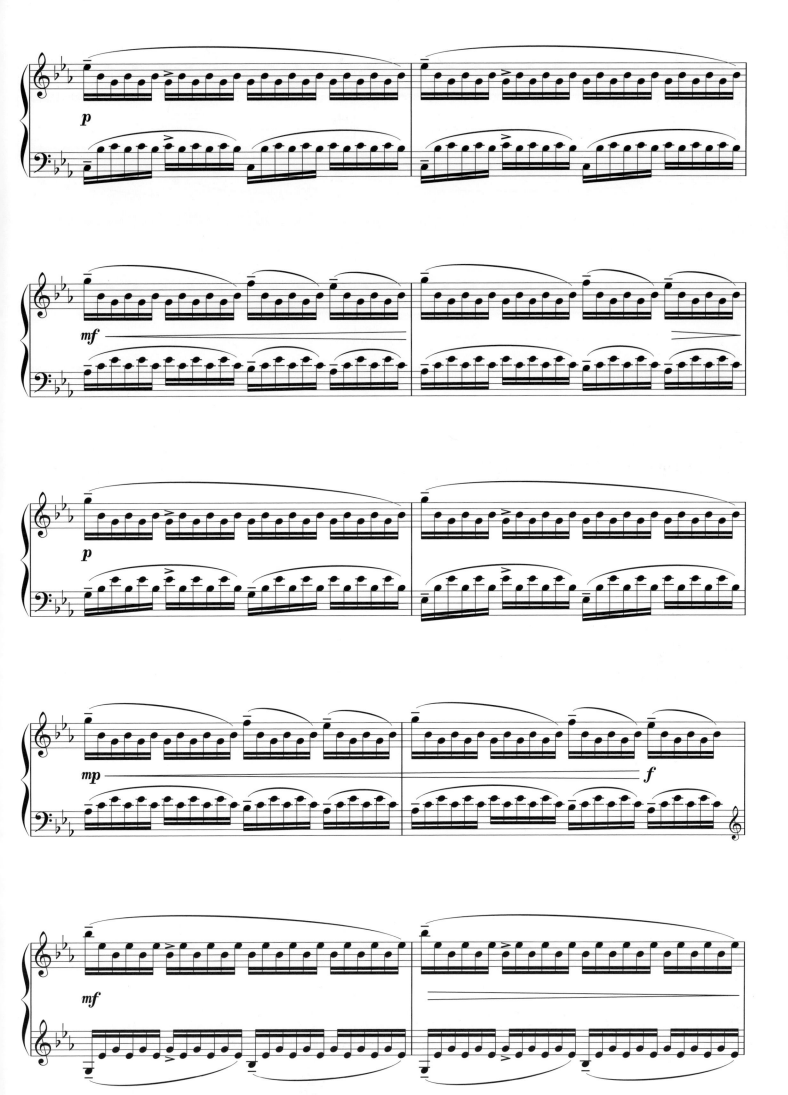

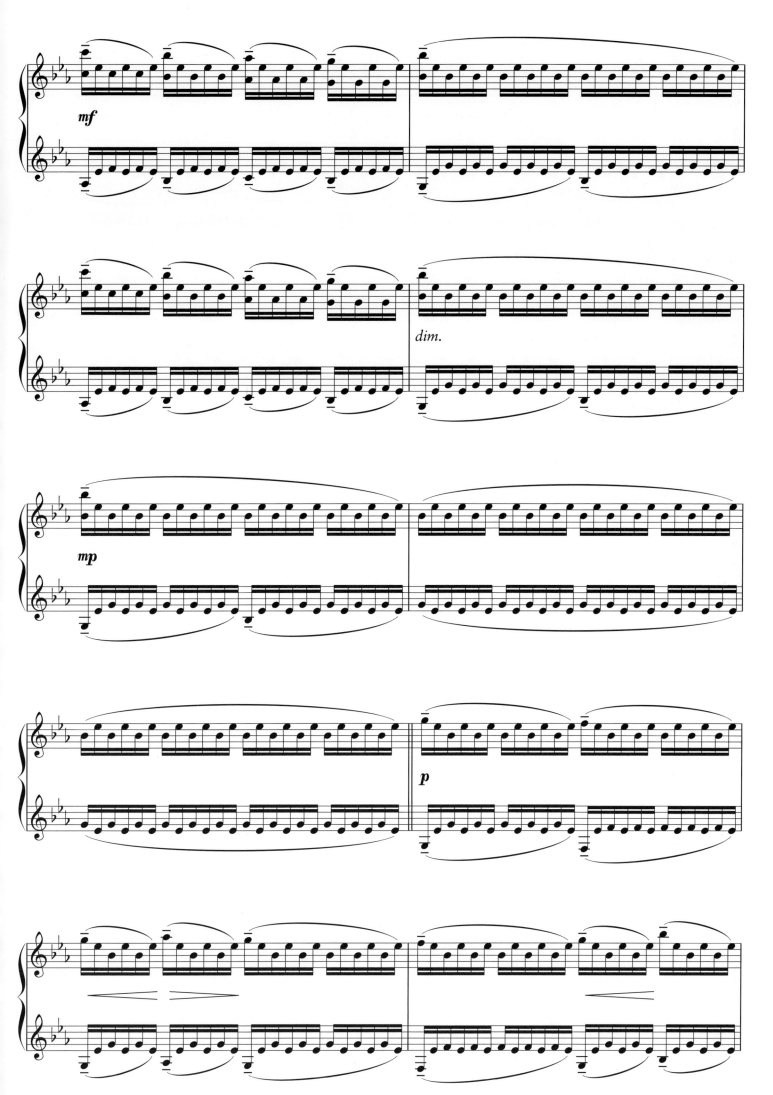

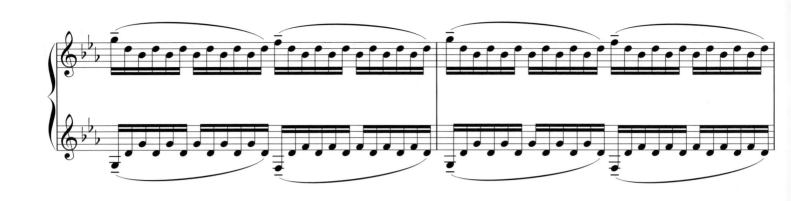

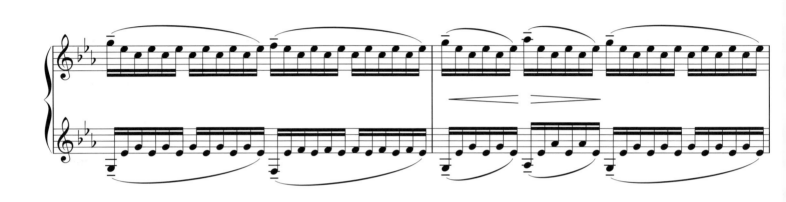

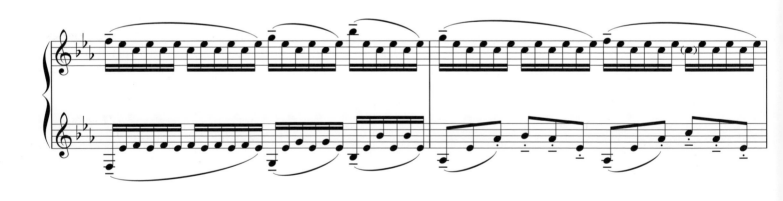

amougen . . . . . . Kentlusk

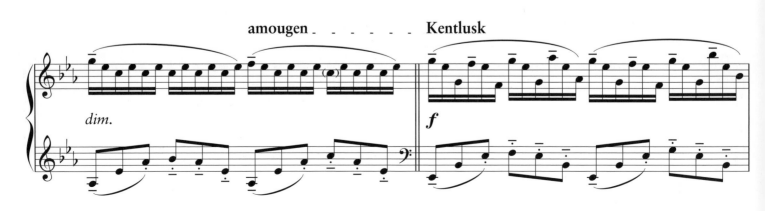

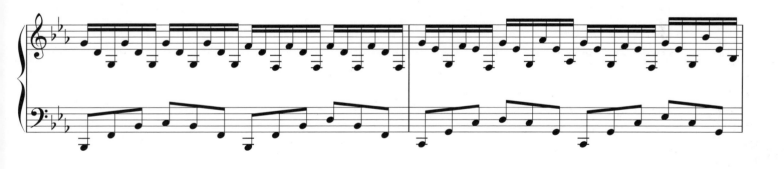

PORZ GORET

48° 26' 19"N 5° 6' 40"W

PORZ GORET

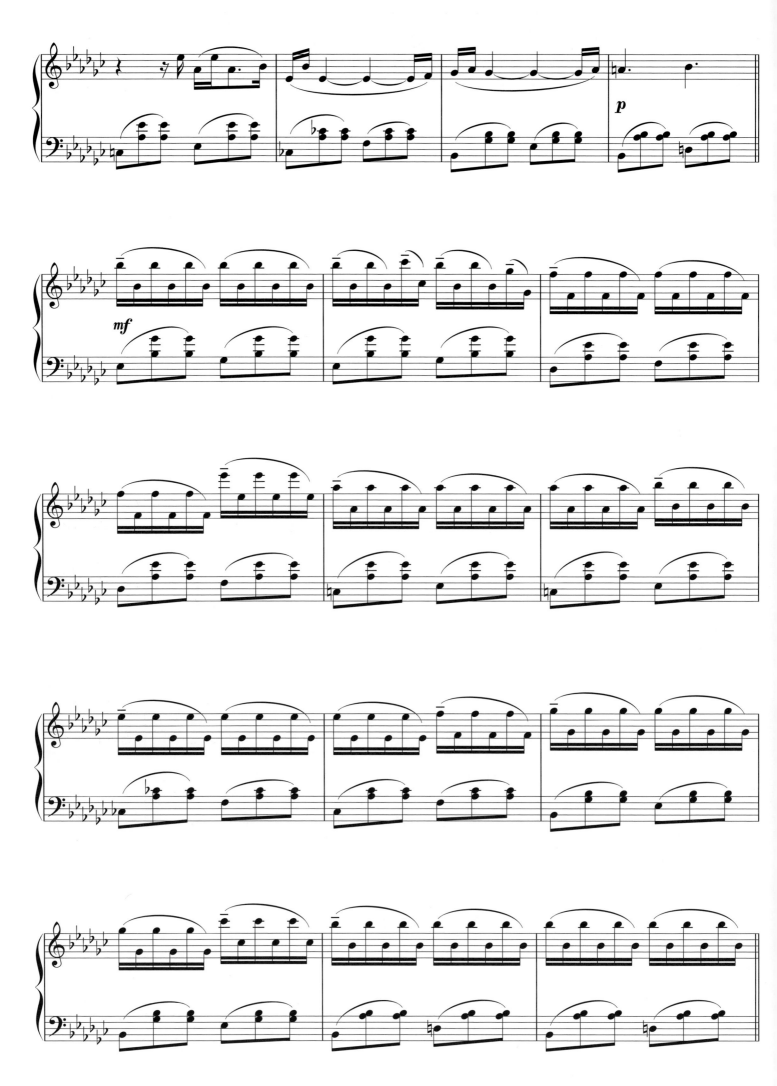

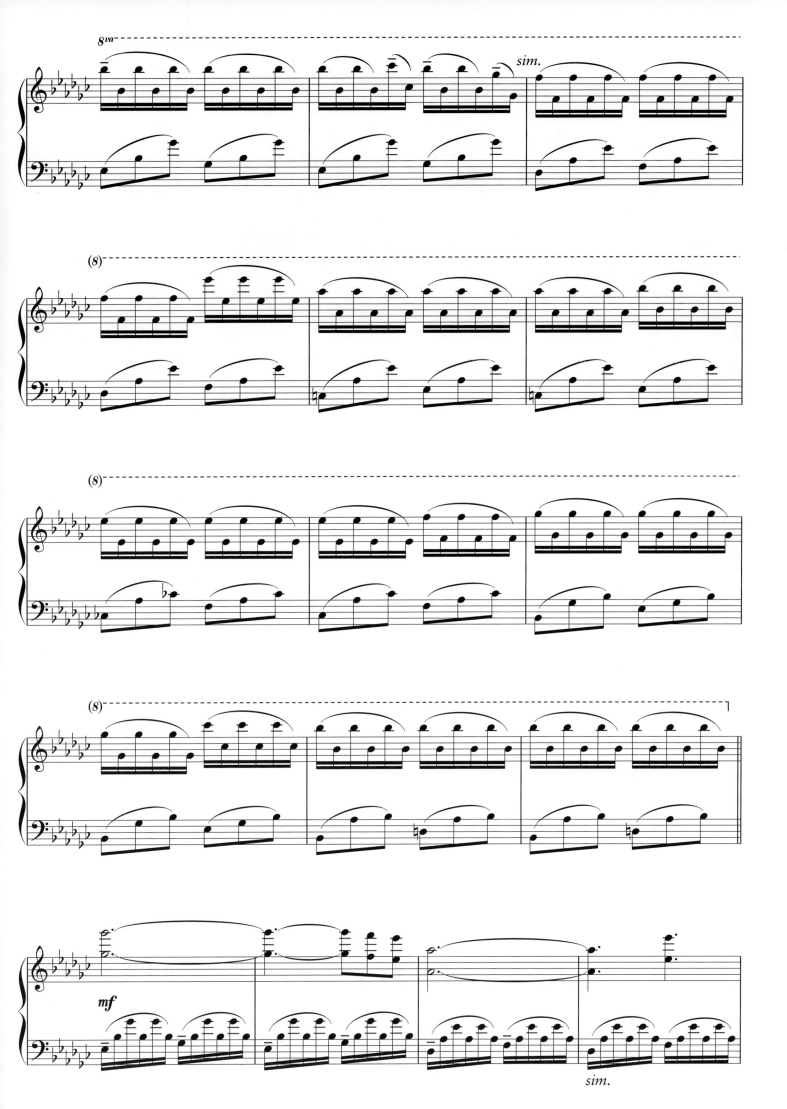

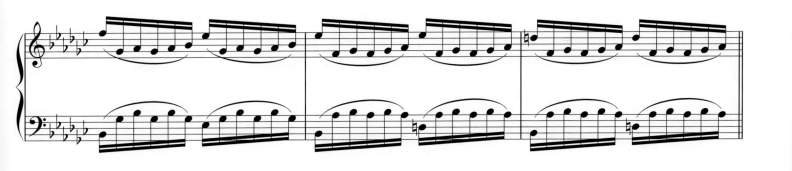

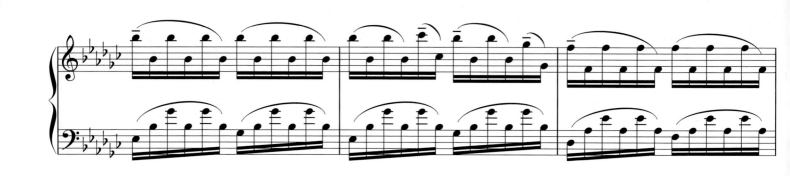

sim.

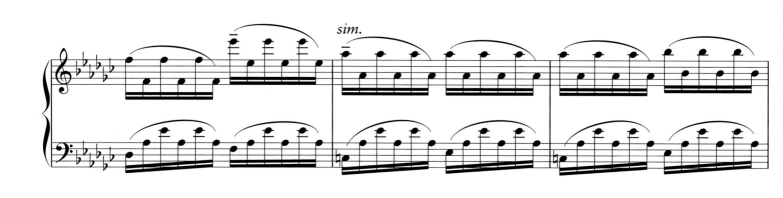

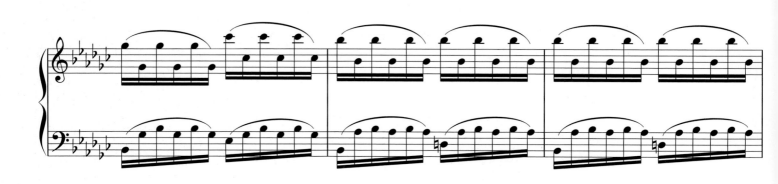

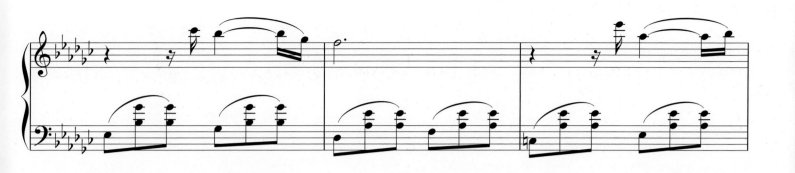

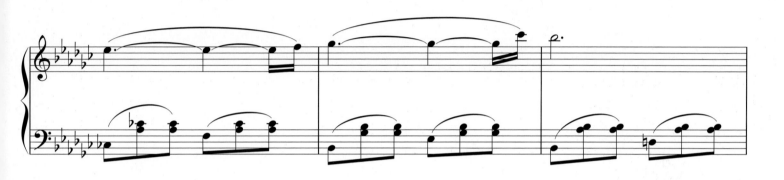

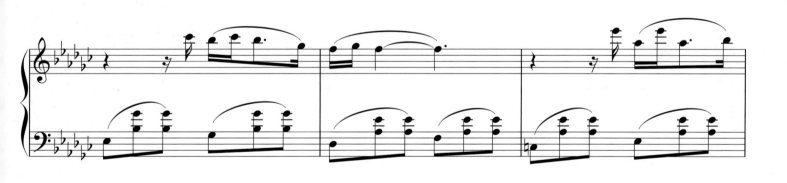

amougen

dasson

LOK GWELTAZ

LOK GWELTAZ

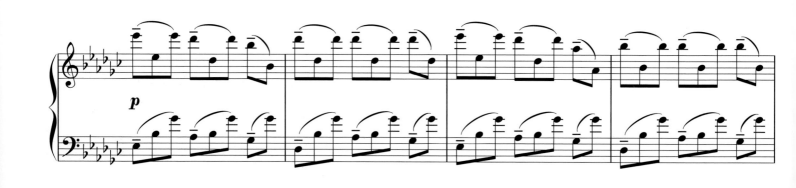

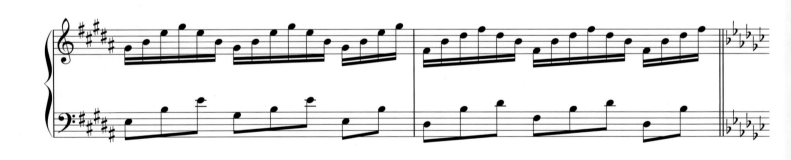

ENN AR ROC'H

48° 27' 22"N 5° 3' 13"W

PENN AR ROC'H

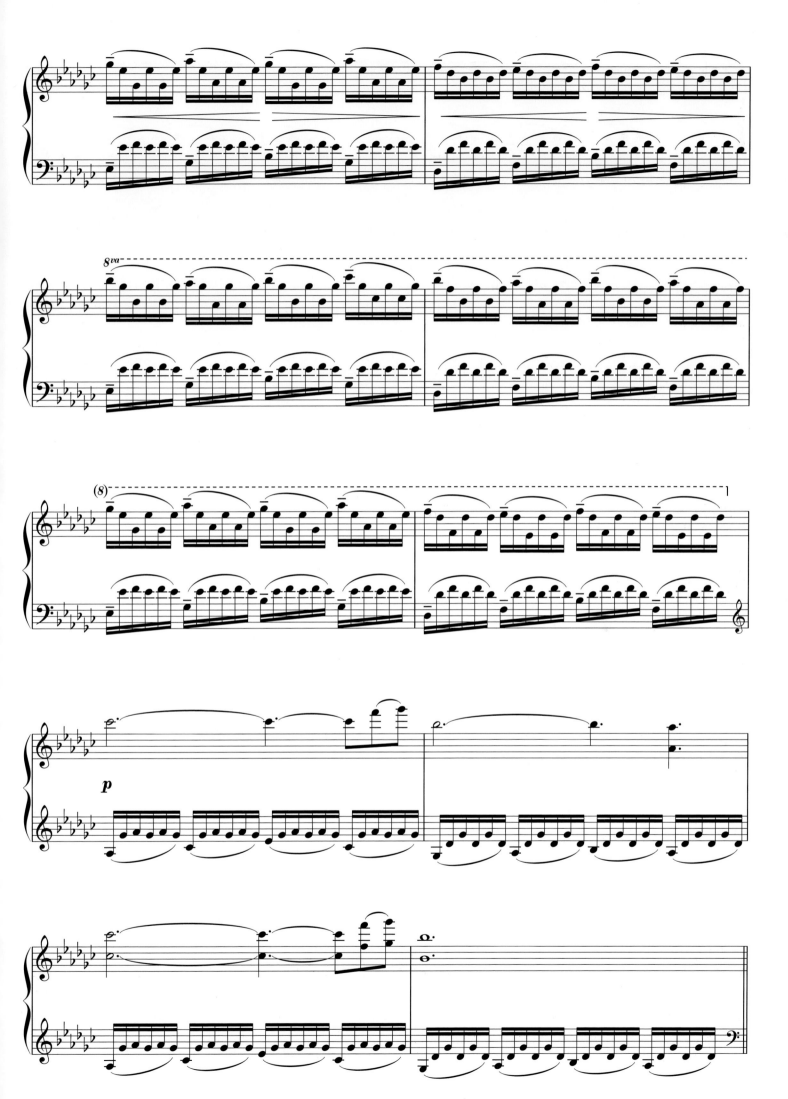

KEREON

gant *Ped.*

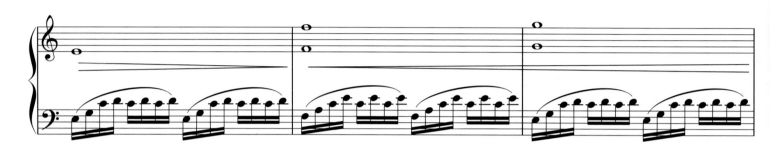

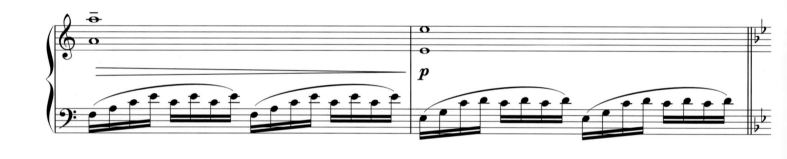

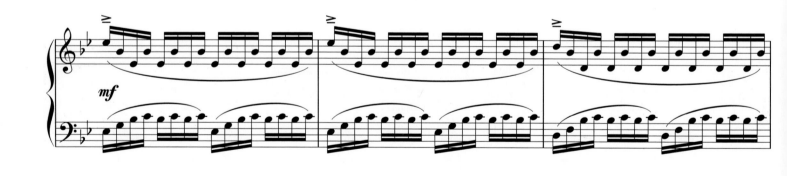

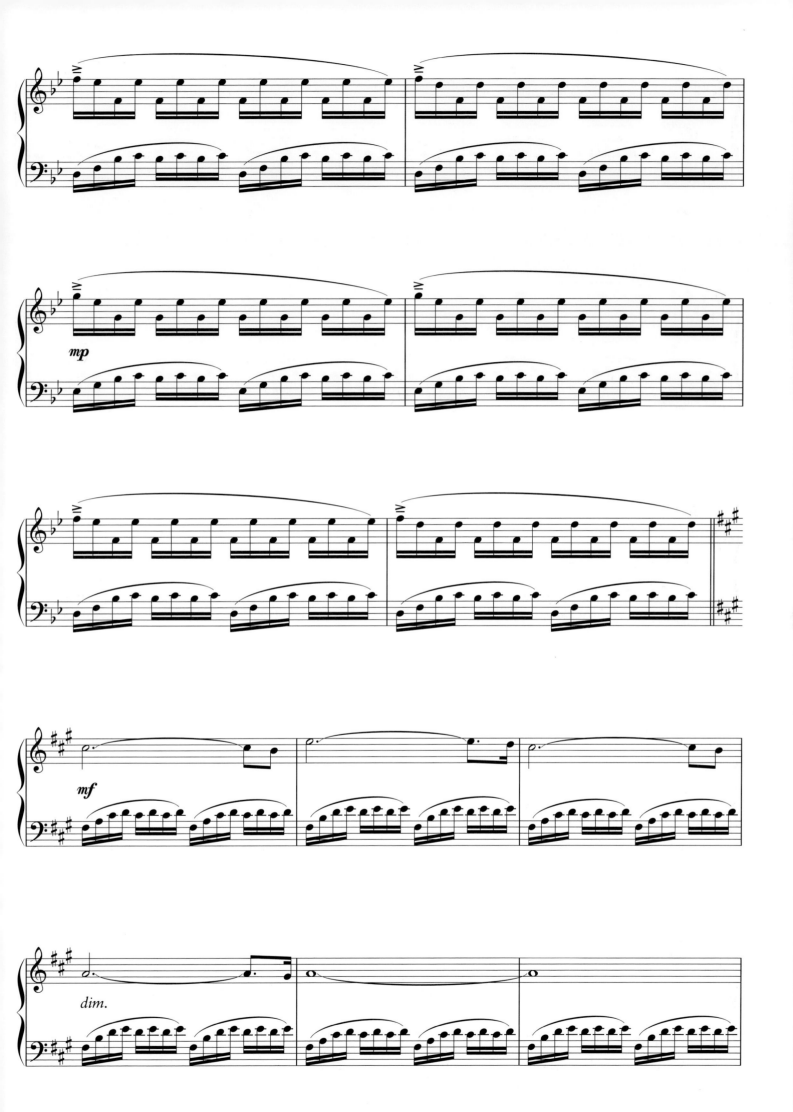

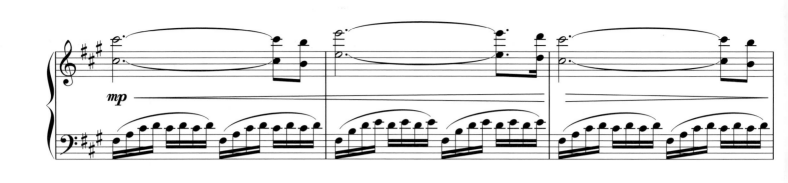

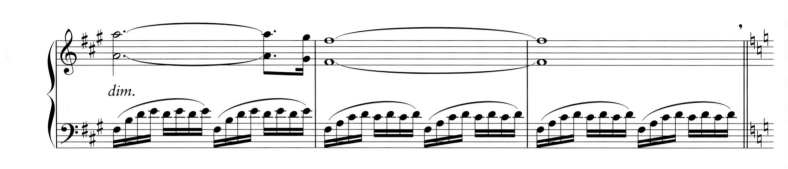

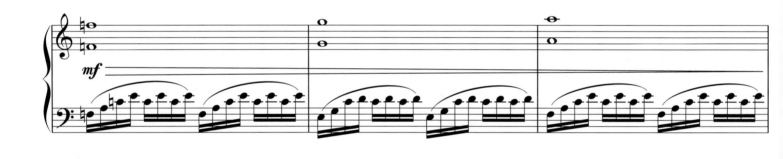

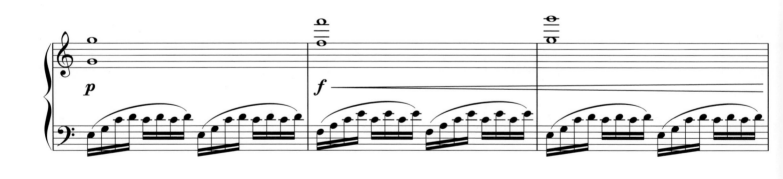

amougen _ _ _ _ _ _ _

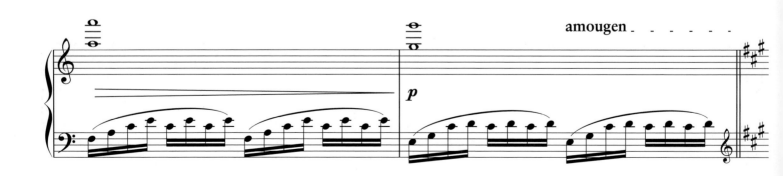

Kentlusk

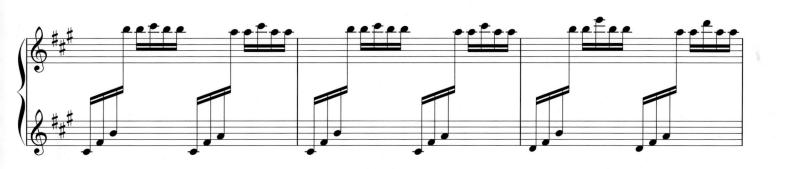

YUZIN

48° 28' 11"N 5° 6' 27"W

YUZIN

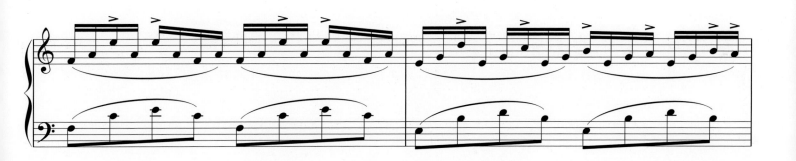

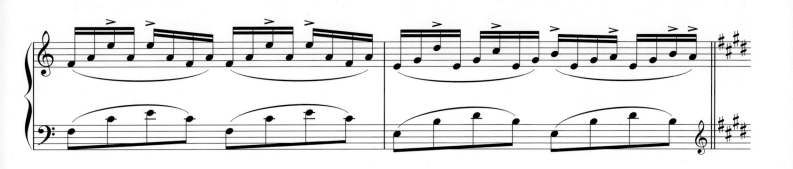

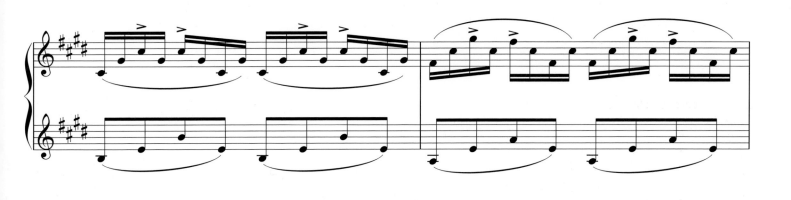

goustadik

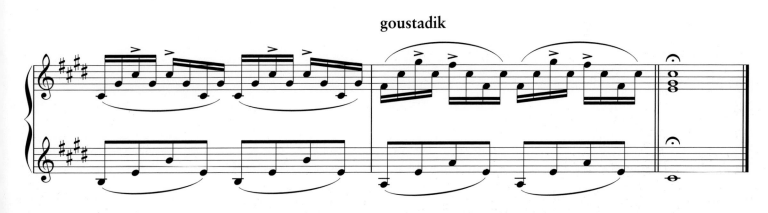

ROC'H AR VUGALE

48°28'22"N 5°6'13"W

ROC'H AR VUGALE

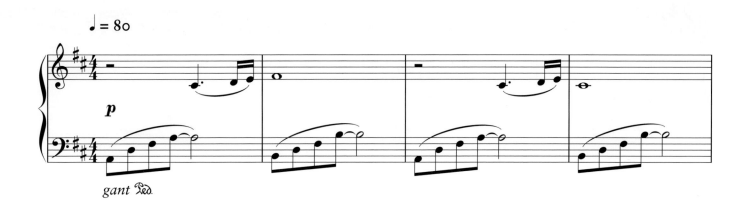

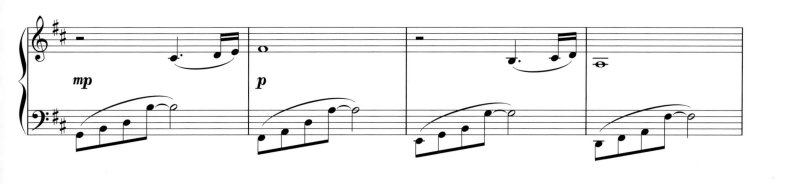

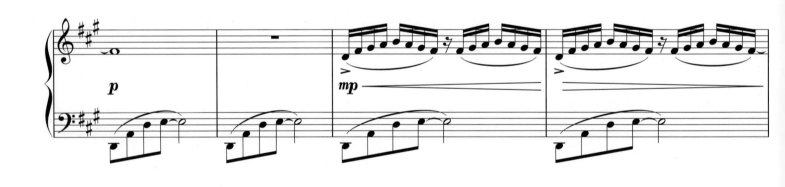

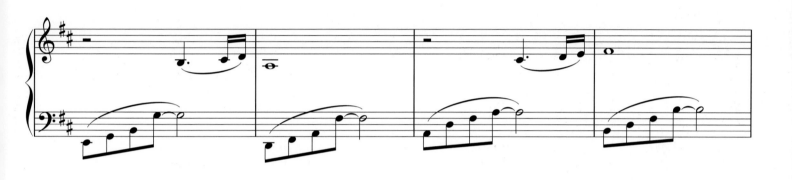

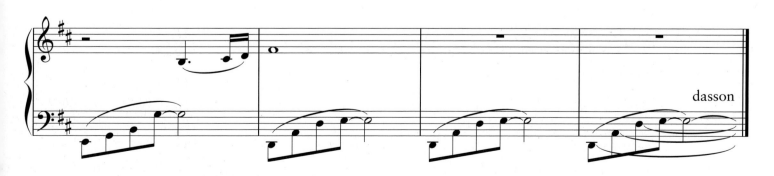

dasson

PENN AR LANN

48°27'46"N 5°2'6"W

PENN AR LANN

ENEZ NEIN

48°27'6"N 5°3'17"W

ENEZ NEIN

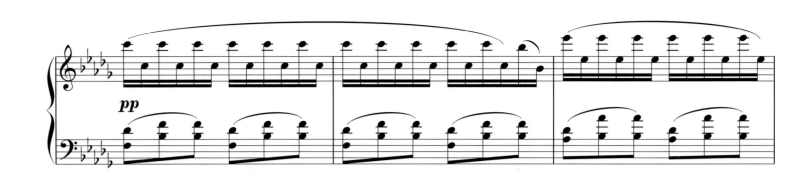

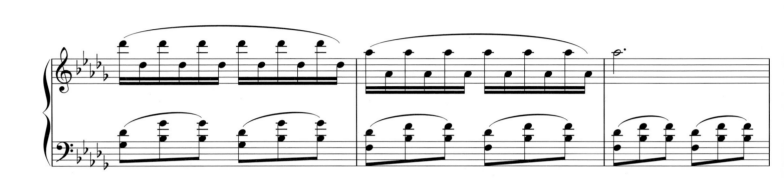

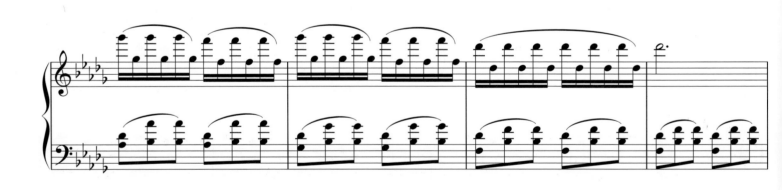

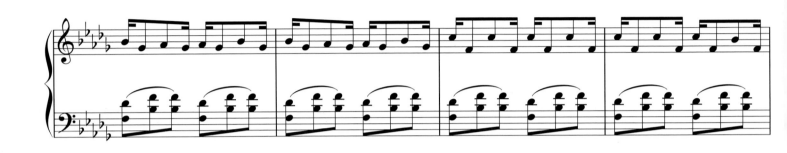

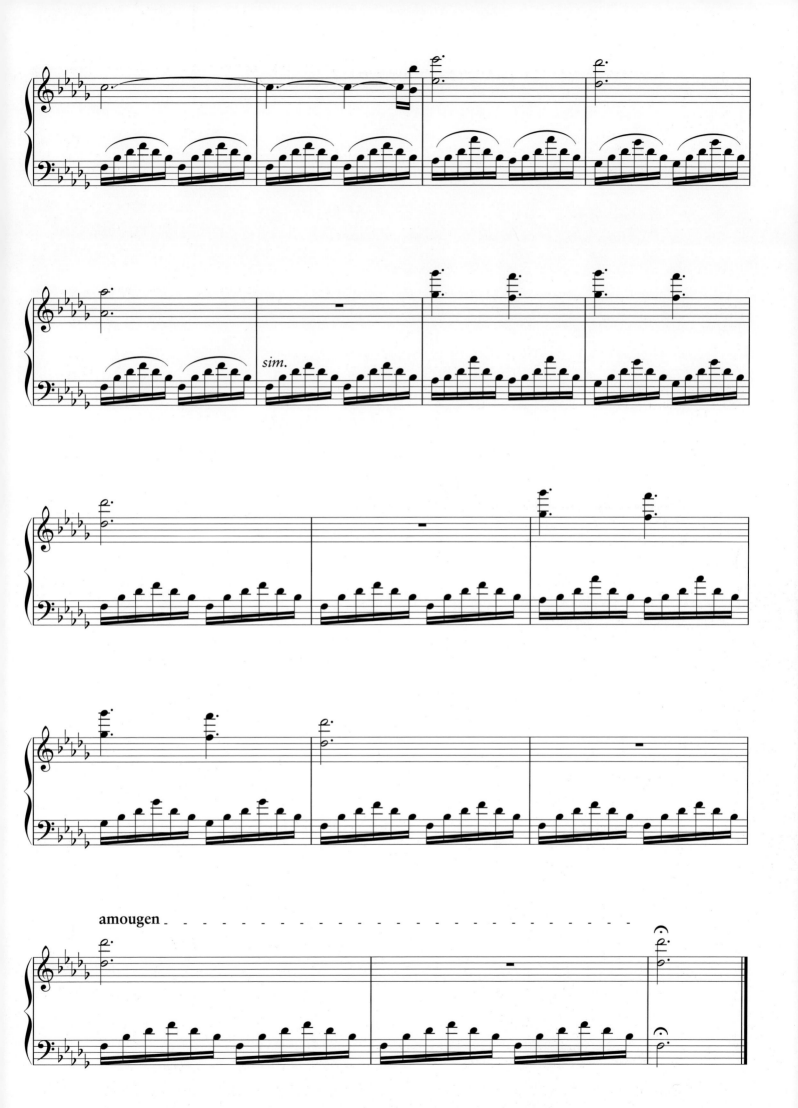

KADORAN

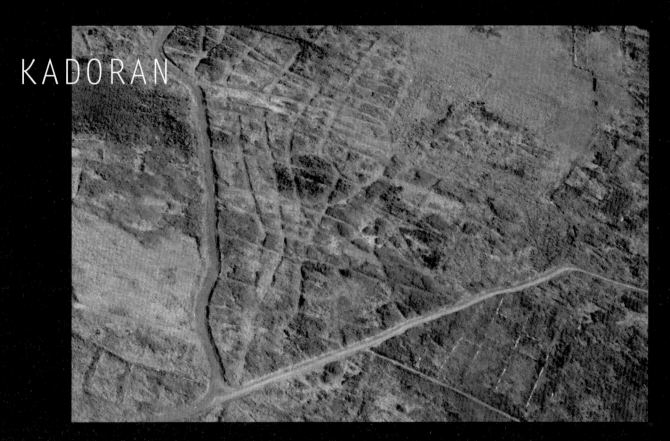

48° 28' 33"N 5° 3' 60"W

KADORAN

amougen = gradually slowing in tempo; *ritardando*.

dasson = with resonance.

gant 𝒫𝑒𝑑. = with pedal.

goustadik = slowly.

kentlusk = first tempo; *tempo primo*.

reollusk = in tempo; *a tempo*.

Setu al liamm evit selaou an enroladennoù
www.eusasound.bzh

Download or stream the ambient backing audio at
www.eusasound.bzh